Who Hears with These Ears?

by Cari Meister

PEBBLE
a capstone imprint

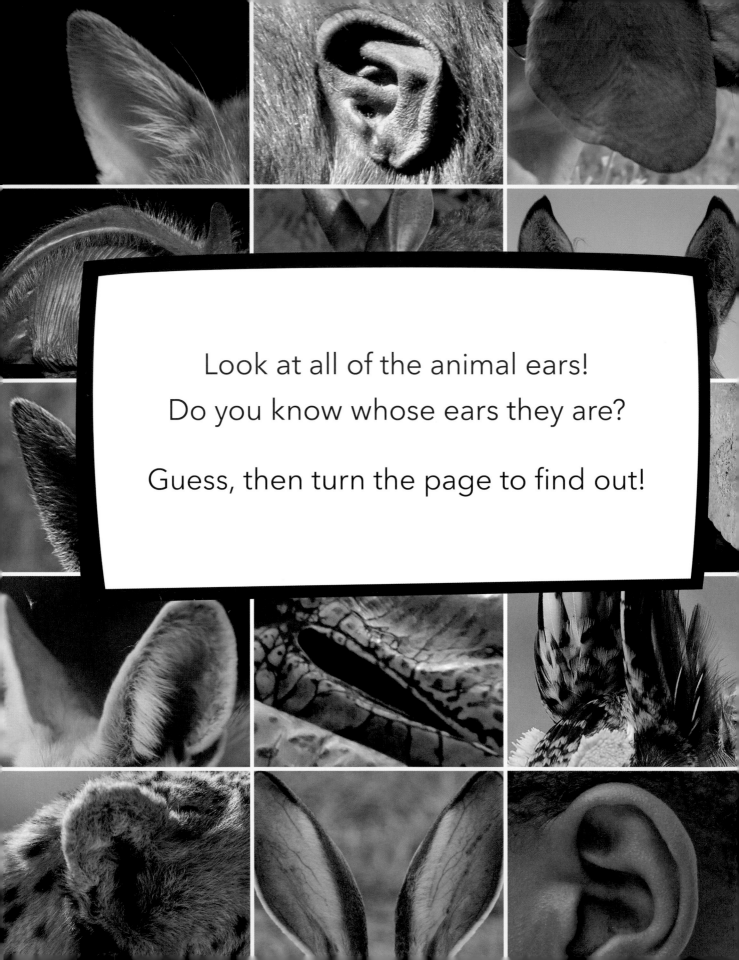

Look at all of the animal ears!
Do you know whose ears they are?

Guess, then turn the page to find out!

Who hears with these ears?

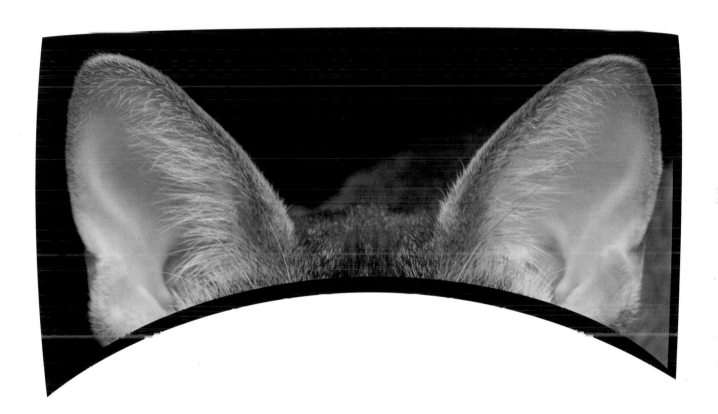

Turn and see!

CAT

Pointy ears form triangles on top of an Abyssinian cat's head.

Who hears with this ear?

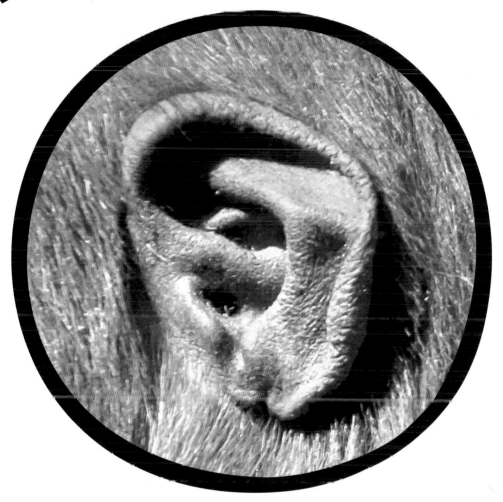

Turn and see!

GORILLA

A gorilla listens for danger in the thick forest leaves.

Who hears with this ear?

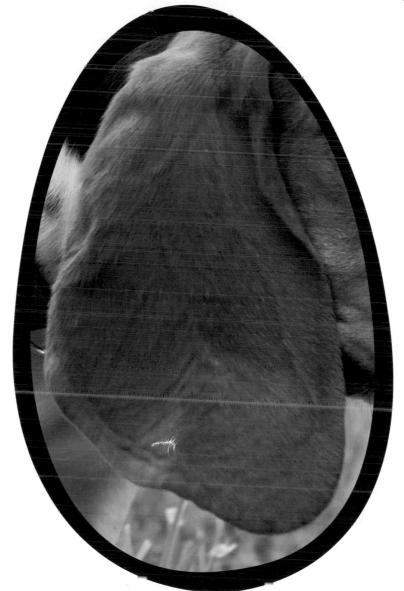

Turn and see!

DOG

A basset hound's long, floppy ears help bring smells to its nose.

Who hears with this ear?

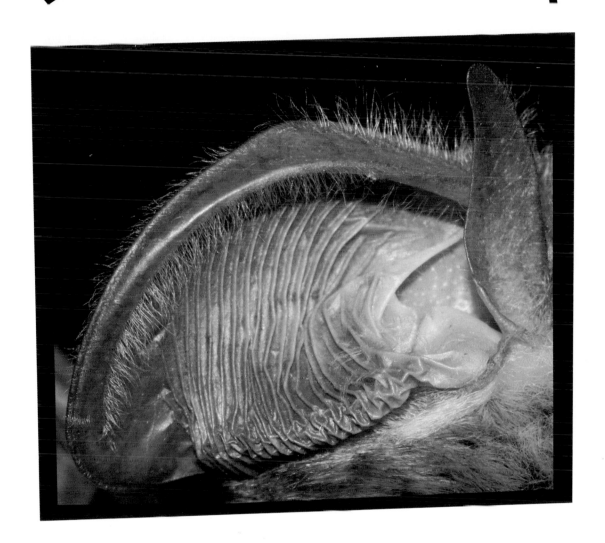

Turn and see!

Who hears with these ears?

Turn and see!

BILBY

Big bilby ears listen for predators in the Australian desert.

Who hears with these ears?

Turn and see!

HORSE

Horse ears turn
back and forth
to pinpoint sounds.

Who hears with these ears?

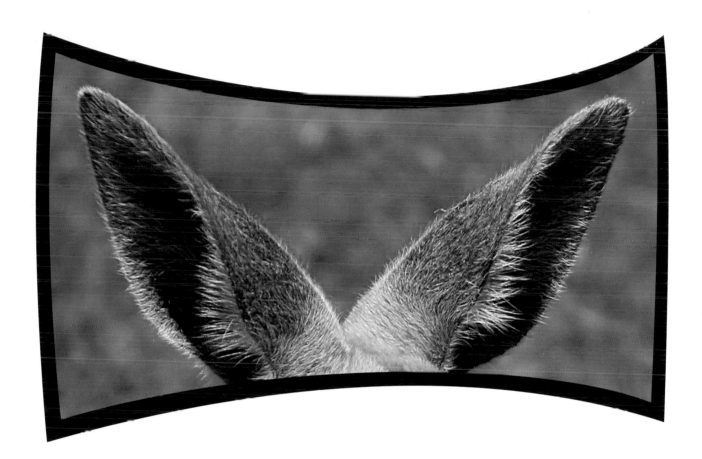

Turn and see!

KANGAROO

Kangaroo ears swivel
toward sounds.

Who hears with this ear?

Turn and see!

ELEPHANT

Giant ears flap to help an elephant stay cool.

Who hears with these ears?

Turn and see!

Fox

A fennec fox's large ears let off heat to keep the animal cool in the hot desert.

Who hears with this ear?

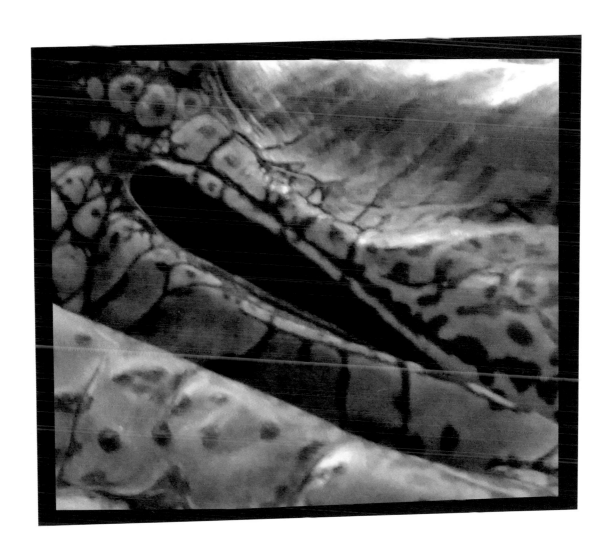

Turn and see!

CROCODILE

A croc's ears seal shut
to keep out water.

Who hears with this ear?

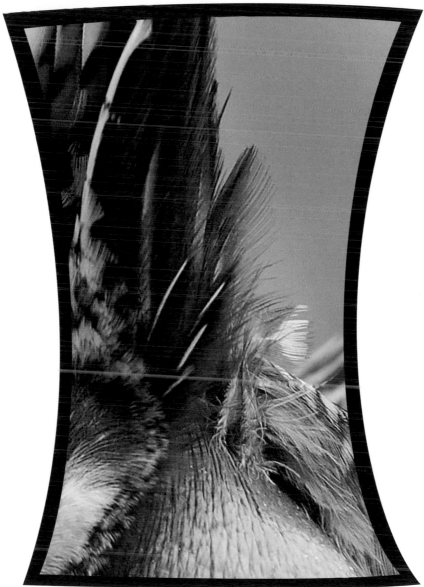

Turn and see!

CHICKEN

Long tufts look like ears, but they are feathers! A prairie chicken hears with tiny ear holes that are hidden under its feathers.

Whose ears are these?

Turn and see!

CHEETAH

Special inner-ear parts help a cheetah keep its head still while sprinting across the ground.

Whose ears are these?

Turn and see!

JACKRABBIT

Tall ears let off
heat and keep a
jackrabbit cool.

Whose ear is this?

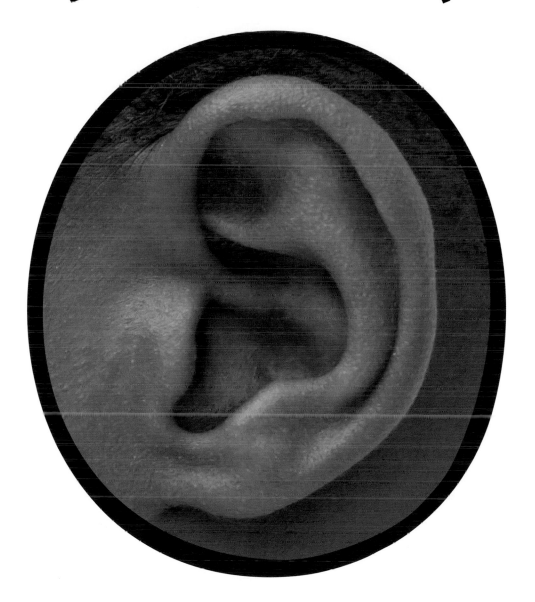

Turn and see!

HUMAN

A child's ears hear
songs and giggles.

Large or tiny, ears help animals hear. They sense danger and help animals stay cool. Ears are amazing!

Pebble Sprout is published by Pebble, an imprint of Capstone.
1710 Roe Crest Drive
North Mankato, Minnesota 56003
www.capstonepub.com

Library of Congress Cataloging-in-Publication Data is available on the Library of Congress website.
ISBN 978-1-9771-2531-6 (library binding)
ISBN 978-1-9771-2541-5 (eBook PDF)
Summary: Grrr! This photo-guessing game challenges pre-readers to guess whose ears are in the images. The furry, floppy, and finely tuned answers may be surprising!

Editor: Shelly Lyons
Designer: Bobbie Nuytten
Media Researcher: Jo Miller
Production Specialist: Katy LaVigne

Image credits
Getty Images: Dave WATTS/Contributor, 11, 12; Shutterstock: Artem Verkhoglyad, 20, Ashley Chapman, 14, Chris Renshaw, 6, Dallen Loest, 7, 8, David Steele, 18, Dennis Forster, 17, DiversityStudio, 29, Dr.Margorius, 3, Ger Bosma Photos, 15, Gucio_55, 10, hagit berkovish, Cover, 19, Ingrid Curry, 28, Isroil, 21, John De Winter, 25, JonathanC Photography, 26, Marianne Purdie, 16, Monkey Business Images, 30, olga_gl, 5, sara fly, 22, Sean R. Stubben, 27, Seregraff, 4, sigurcamp, 13, Stephen M, 9, Steve Oehlenschlager, 23, 24

Design Elements
Capstone; Shutterstock: Artishok, cajoer, Fourleaflover, linear_design, srikorn thamniyom

Printed and bound in China.
3322

Good job! Try all the books in this series!